Standing Tall

By Debbi Brawner

Standing Tall
Copyright © 2021 Debbi Brawner

ISBN-13: 979-8722041326

Dedication

I want to dedicate this book to my children
Cody, and Micheal. I would be nothing without you. I
have had many challenges with you but never did I want
to give up.
You challenge me to just be alive.

Love always, mom
Thank you

The Demon

I dreamed of the days long ago
But those days are long gone
If you cared you would do
However, you choose to go on

I wish you could see
The pain you caused
Only you can decide to
feed the demon that does

The demon only comes out when you choose
You were always there
Now you always loose
Lost to the hereafter

I plead for you to be
Be that guy that never did
The guy that could see
See beyond what could be off the grid

We were so much alike
Although that has changed
Because you choose the demon out of spite
We are forever strained

Truth

Your life has taken you so far
From this land and beyond
As we were and as we are
We have such a bond look

Your pain is such a burden
Mine is not
I wished it could be transferred
Only to be a thought

You never have a doubt
Because you know it's true
We will be there no matter what
If our time takes us without due

I will never take it as truth
Because only you
Can make it worth
The ride we take it through

It amazes me how
How it could be so long
But I only now
You have brought it along

My First

I would have never dreamed
That you cold
But you were so clean
Never thought I would

You would have so much to give
I gave you my everything
Only to see you live
And to grow so big

You were my first
But wouldn't be my last
I could never rehearse
And never ask

You were perfect
Head to toe
I checked
And always a glow

To this day
I am so proud
To say
It out loud

His Tears

His ignorance
So fresh
However, the world is not
He looks to for the rest
As he looks to us to not get caught

What do we teach
Manners, dignity, or respect
Is it all out of reach
Or is it up to subject

Mine are grown
However, he is not
Because it's a long shot

His tears
Are heartbreaking
And in the coming years
He will be the decision-maker

Actions

I wondered
Wondered why
So I ponder
But how there's no need to cry

You have made me feel
Feel like I am nothing
I feel like I could kill
Because I am not trusting

You have chosen
The ones that are most valuable
And to me, that seems broken
You will never be rational

I feel so conflicted
But why
Cuz' you are the one addicted
I am left to justify

Justify your actions
Then, now, Tomorrow
All I see is your distractions
My eyesight is no longer narrow

Deceived

You have broken my heart yet again
I wanted it to change
But how could that be with all the pain
We were so much estranged

It felt like it could be
And again I was deceived
Because as you can see
She is not to be believed

I wished could, I wished I might
Say it isn't so
She goes off into the night
And I cry out no

It never changes with time
Because she could not
If it were a crime
She would never be caught

Our days on this Earth are numbered
If she only knew
The pain shifted
To me, it will be too few

Me Too

I think of you every day
I'm told to forget
And so I say
Don't judge me for what he did

What you did was
Take my ignorance
What you did was take my innocence

You live your life nothing happened
Every day I struggle
Although I am saddened
I have grown to be humble

So less and less I think of you
But do I forget
I wonder how many more can say me too
So I say to you, you are no longer a threat

Scars

I bear the scars you can not see
Although you seemed pleased
I never let it be
I fought and scraped to be free

You never saw me for what I did
Only what you needed
I never said
However you always pleaded

Always remembering how it was
Not to repeat it
Was the fact that I loved
But to you I never was fit

I often wondered how
But only knew
That one day I would be out
And you too

Now I am out
Not without the scars
With a new sense of doubt
That only one day I would be afar

New

Up to the moment I met you
I was overjoyed
You were brand new
But I could never be afraid

We were together
But you were so appeasing
I would be your fair weather
You would always want to be pleasing

We grew so close
I could not let go
Even now That everyone knows
You will always be in tow

So now that we made it
Every breath brand new
You will always have my heart
Because together we grew

One day we will be gone
But for you
It will move on
And you will have it all, I knew

Safe Haven

We were so close
But the years
And miles between us
Something so feared

You went your way
Me, mine
Forever we're afraid
But together fine

As we believe we would
Our lives o share
We thought we could
Never be scared

At the end of our days
We will be forgiven
Until we part ways
I will be forever your safe haven

Fate

I believe in fate
So that's why I have you
We become soulmates
But only you understand a few

We are given a challenge in life
Our challenge was each other
I became your wife
It is about one another

Our ideas were combined
How can you not see my struggle
You are not lying
I don't want to be a bother

See

Always from the start
I believed in you
As for one day, we would part
Many would do

The hurt
The harder it got
I was mi=ore and n=more blurred
And forever sought

Not to believe
Was never a choice
But to receive
Never a noise

You deliver day after day
Many will see
Your word does say
He will be your light forever to be

Now You Can

You were to keep me safe and sound
But that was not so
I want to be underground
Even though you glow

We would play
Ashamed
As we were misled
Only this guy was your aim

You often chose another
However, we would still need
The need was bother
It was the bother we seek

Although we seek
The more you ran
You ran because you were weak
But now we both can

Need You Now

Many need you
As did I
But as you do what you do
So many die

Not for a cause
But because you are warm
However, you won't ever pause
Because you cause so much harm

The more you grow
The smaller I become
Because I can not let you go
You have a hold and I am numb

Regardless of time
You never quit
But for me, you are gone
The pain you will never get

I have to let you go
But for so many
You will always grow
We are worth more than a penny

Depart

The animosity you a=show
And in the same place
We are to grow
I often want to race

Race to the door
But that door does not appear
Only because we were
We were so near

All I want is
To be so close
When all I get
Is a noise

However, I seemed to be
The only noise
Although I want to see
She only to close

A closed-door
A closed mind
Only to depart
Departing seems to be so kind

Keep You

You didn't have to but you did
I took you for mine
We often said
You are my sunshine

Although we took we each other
Every day of the week
You get me further and further
In so deep

As the days go by
I often wonder why
We don't surrender

Surrender to blood
Because
I need you more and more
Our feelings flood
More than what we ask for

Never was forced
Only to keep
Keep each other
In our dreams

See You Go

My pleasure quickly becomes a pain
As I watch you go
Only to see you again
My only desire is to see you so

My mind often wanders
To you
I can only surrender

No distance of time can lessen our friendship
Who are thoroughly persuaded beach other's worth
Off my lip
I can assure it on Earth

Though the miles may be between us
We are never apart
For our friendship doesn't count miles
It is measured by heart

My heart belongs to you
For you to do at your will
We will always be two
Because we can always and will always fulfill

Prove

It has never ceased to amaze me
The way you have changed
By the way
I have aged

You have challenged
My every move
Not only the knowledge
But to prove

Prove me wrong
Or prove me right
It's in our song
But in my sight

I have never been more proud
You show me every day
I can be in the clouds
And you show me every way

Fallen Star

We dreamed of a better life
However, it seems like it was just that
Because we had so much strife
To arrive at

We fought and screamed
But it never was so
That we leaned
Leaned into it more

The more we grew
It became so clear
That we knew
We had to compare

As of now
We are so far apart
But somehow
It can only start

Start from where
To end up where we are
It is all a blur
We can only wish upon a star

Reminded

I ask for so much
And got so little
Wanting your touch
Having to settle

As you would decide
Decide our fate
Only to collide
It was too late

Believing your words
Was not to be so
Because it wasn't worth
Worth it to close

We have since forgiven
That path has not been paved
To listen
We not easily carved

Often reminded
I can only accept
Always the Mastermind
I will never forget

Not Prepared

Your pain I have not felt
I know I will
You have often said
How bad it feels

Yours was so close
Mine was far away
We were to lose
But I am afraid

As we all do
I am not prepared
You have said so
And I am scared

I have forgiven
You have lost
We all know you will be leaving
As you are called

When that happens
We will not be scared
But will be saddened
When you are paired

Her

I tried to keep you as long as I could
You are now to be free
We have often looked
But could never let it be

Now belong to another
As we all now know
However, Sadder that will never smother
Because it is so

We see each other every day
You have her
In every way
I am so glad to see it as it was

She has now become mine
For this I am blessed
Because you make him shine
He is at his best

Hope He Can

I believe you want peace
But for that to happen
He has to believe in me
His thoughts wonder how I can listen

He only hears what I tell
For that, I have to be open
All I want to do is yell
And scream into the ocean

If I only could
Maybe just might be so
He often thinks you would
But he could never know

His pain is so great
How do I describe
Described
It to him at length
The aftermath of my life

Our lives now
Are full of our boys
But the old if it won't go
I can only hope that he stays

Hard Fought

I often think the way it was
And believe now
We had it just because
Our heads were in the clouds

We would dream
Of the way it could be
And prayed for a change
Because we long to be free

As of now we both are still chained
Although not because of her
But because we are sane
We have not been heard

Screamed out in pain
And we want that love
But our love is in vain
Yell to God above

We wanted it so bad
Never in our reach
It could not be sadder
In your world, it is just a figure of speech

If I could
I wouldn't
Only because it would
Be so hard-fought

Your Ring

The love we have is like no other
We started like so many
Then I was undercover
Now I have plenty

Not in money
Not a lack of love
Only every day being sunny
And having a helping hand from above

We have had our battles
But has never broke
We were rattled
But we always spoke

You gave me so much
And I you
Count on your touch
Even though it may have been a zoo

In the end, we came together
Our little family has grown so big
And with that, I wanted no other
I will always have your ring

Imagine

Dear God, please
Don't take her from us
With her at ease
It breaks me up

Don't let her goodbye
Be our last
If only our lives
Had been our past

But God you see
She's everything to me
Who will be
Known to me like a lock fits a key

I can't imagine
It's all over
Because if anyone can
You have that power

Time

Our path in life is uncertain
We can go it alone
Or we can be determined
And go through it with someone

Our love is undeniable
But for some reason, it feels forced
Only because it can be justifiable
I feel like I might burst

Your love is all I needed
Can you see
Even if I pleaded
I think not because you want to be free

Were we meant to be
Or have we wasted our time
My satisfaction would be a crime

Regrets

I thought I had you
Your heart and soul
I have found that is not so
I have never felt so low

You had every part of me
From start to finish
Why can't you see
What I can't seem to diminish

We have grown so close
But drifted so far away
My heart is froze
I wish you could stay

It seems the harder I fight
The harder it gets
I want to right
All you want is no regrets

The Cost

God has a plan for us
Whether we know it or not
For you, I can only guess
Find yourself in a knot

If you were to believe
That only if
It could be
What would be so phony

They have you
However, they are lost
Unless given a clue
No matter the cost

What more do I have to give
What else does he have to take
To what extent do you have to live
Until you wake

We can not see
But for us
It is not free
And for all of you have to do is trust

Eluded

You elude me so much
But I will seek you out
However long it takes for your soft touch
We are forever in doubt

I need you
You need me not
It seems you are brand new
You are within eyeshot

The more I fight
The more you forget
Everything is so bright
Though I sometimes get

You never seem to care
There were plenty of times I need you
Because you are so rare
I do hope we can finally make a breakthrough

Chance

We met as a chance
And survived apart
But never gave it a chance
Because we have heart

It became love
Only by choice
All above
I have your voice

You were there for me
When no others were
However only at my plea
It occurs

Without our chance to meet
I would never have you
So for now I will not beat
Because of you, I am true

Called

More and more every day
I think of you and then
In each and every way
We go on as we possibly can

My thoughts wonder as to how
How we have to move on
Someday somehow is now
That we have the new dawn

The dawn is what we seek
Because of you, we dream
Dream that dream so we are not weak
YOu believed in us so it seemed

One day we will see
See that you are never gone
We will have to let it be
That you were the one called upon

Wonder

We wander through the night
Like we are blind
I want to see you in my sight
It is not so kind

You believe in me
But I never made it easy
For you to see
My heart is not so pleasing

Because we have
We have none
You survive
Because of one

For that one
We have to plead
But the plea is not free
We deliver the need

The need is great
So great I want you
I want you to wait
Wait for it to be brand new

Need

You gave me your heart
I never knew
But being apart
What was I to do

As we often do
You never seem to hear
That I need you
Need you dear

We look for the payoff
I still need your word
However, must you put me off
I am still not heard

Only this once could you please
Please give me what I need
With such ease
One day I know we can succeed

Stop the Clock

Time standstill
But the clock moves on
I am at your will
We were only like one

You gave me the intensity
Of being me
However, you saw my curiosity
It only increases with my glee

I want the clock to stop
If only for a minute
That minute being on top
Not for it to go up and up

We go around in this life
A lifetime of pain
Me as your wife
I want it again and again

Does it seem
That our time is now
If that clock will let us dream
We can somehow

In Mourning

The grief I feel
Will never be seen
But always will
Keep itself unforeseen

Although the years have passed
It never leaves
I am embarrassed
However, you believe

You often creep into my thoughts
The belief that I could
Or that I could not
Believe that you would

You would finally leave
But for that to happen
It could not be received
To receive I would always be saddened

Sadden because
I never got a warning
My thoughts
Turn to be in mourning

Superstar

You look to us for insight
For love
Or just for the light
From up above

Your hair the color of the sun
Your eyes the color of the sky
You have so much fun
As you float like a butterfly

We often are distracted
By the hours of the day
Our wish has been granted
Because you are often the one that shows us the way

You will become our future
But for now, you are our sweetheart
As you show us your humor
One day you will be our superstar

New Heights

Your eyes and heart are saddened
But you have to let go
Let go of the hard
The anger that grows

Your smile is contagious
All to contemplating
We laugh as if we were teenagers
Can he really be that manipulating

If you could see
What I see
You wouldn't be
So easy to hear my plea

If we could
Would you ask
Ask yourself if your livelihood
Worth the mask

We are not meant to be alone
Can it be worth the price
Having your feet held to the firestone
Or will you soon have new heights

Carefree

When I looked into your eyes
All I see is desire
Like a firefly
Your hopes and dreams are a high flyer

With all your might
And all your heart
You will always be right
But never will you fall apart

Your eyes swell with pride
As we see you grow
You take life in stride
We want you to take it slow

I hope and pray
That you see
See how much there is no despair
And always be carefree

Settle

I call out your name
Over, over and over
But who's to blame
You want all the power

We want it to change
However, no one takes the time
Who are we to cringe
Because it is me that has to climb

Why are you are never wrong
We go through life with a purpose
So why do you have to be so headstrong
It will always surface

To me, my life is not a scramble
Not because of you, please
But because I am humbled
To be forgotten is not easy

The clue to life is not seen
It is not felt
Not absent
Do we have to settle for what we are dealt

Not to Cry

Is it me or is it you
You make me doubt
Only he will know
How our world fades out

We were once close
So close that we could be one
You have to choose
To be outdone

But why
What have I done
Not to cry
Because that is not fun

Will, we ever have it again
Only time will tell
As for now I have to abstain
I have to be well

Without you
I feel lost
Good for you, you have no clue
There will always be a cost

Brand New

Just as I expected
As you and I
Are tested
We often wonder why

You from one place
Me from another
But in either case
We had to discover

Not each other
The warmth you had
The ground we had to cover
Either way, it couldn't go bad

All these years
I still have you
My life being greater
Because every day is brand new

Betrayal

Your betrayal hurts
So I ask myself why
From the heart
My eyes are not dry

Never again you say
However never does
Because from you it is always grey
Not the water but the mud

No matter what he says
It will never change
But from me, it has always
Been strange

Will he win
Or will I
For now, all I can do is grin
Because it does no good to cry

Stand Strong

How this all turns out
We will soon see
You want to shout
But how can that be

Because it's another's decision
That comes with time
Will she listen
Or will she see

Be as it may
May it cost her
In the end, she will say
Say it just to be there

Staying strong
Because it won't be forever
But it won't be long
It will be at your cost

From Above

We depend on each other
For love, acceptance, touch, or just to be happy
But why bother
I would gladly

He's been hurt before
So why would he try
It's hard to ignore
He such a good guy

But ask yourself why not
Never blue sky
Always in your thought
Never with a tear in my eye

His eyes are full of your love
And never let him go
Everything we have comes from above
So that's all we can show

Every Time

Will it be today
Or will it be tomorrow
Even then which way
Do we go

You say left
I say right
But what if it's a cliff
What if it's Rainbow Brite

Either way
We will see
How he has your day
Because I know you are with me

It never ceased
To amaze me
You can with ease
Just to say please

I am sorry
Just isn't enough sometimes
But don't worry
Cuz I will take it every time

Angels

Can we live without love
What about hope
You showed me how to be proud of
Even though we may be walking a tightrope

My love for you will always be
And yours for me
How can we see
Without our plea

Mine would be to never let go
Yours would be not to leave
Just say it isn't so
Because it has to be

Our lives were never parallel
But in our dreams
We have always been real
Nothing is as it seems

When it changes
I don't know
All I can think of is the angels
That will be full of sorrow

Open

Life gives us a lot of blows
As long as I have you
No one will ever know
Why we never knew

Our love grows more and more
I am glad I found you
You rock me to the core
But did we ever know

Know the reason why
Know the reason how
However, we can have it now

But what is it
What is it we have
We can't just sit
We have to learn to save

My love is greater than a river
Greater than the ocean
So you have to deliver
Because I am not settling for anything more

Regardless

You are my angel
That's why I didn't see you until now
It is so painful
Why is it allowed?

We have so many questions
With no answer
You left me with a great impression
But damn that cancer

If not for the circumstances
We would be so fortunate
What if we did an Indian war dance
We could make a great argument

So why would anything work
Because he has a plan
That we can't possibly hit the mark
Even if that plan lessons our lifespan

Why can't we be that pebble
We throw into the river
We will level
Because he will deliver

The Aggression

Here we go again
My thoughts will always come back to you
We weren't meant to go it alone
But it seems that is what I have chosen

Our paths collide every day
However, now that is not so
We never knew the way
Together it was often a stone's throw

I ask myself why
But I know that question
Why cry
Because of the aggression

Is overflowing
More now than ever
Only if we were going
We could measure

Going at it without you
Is debilitating
We were always two
As it is we are always going to be waiting

The Ember

Our lives will never be the same
Because of that day
The love we couldn't contain
It wasn't even halfway

Now can never be compared
To the destiny
It is nothing to be impaired
Because we have a legacy

As you get older
I want you to slow down
That is what I told her
Sometimes you act like a clown

On my final day
Always remember
It's not grey
But the ember

Everyday

Our lives go on every day
You with your
I want it my way
But what about before

Before now
What can we say
I don't know-how
Because we have paved the way

Was the road rocky
Without a doubt
Either way, it is shocking
What to do without that

Our paths continue
How it is paved
How do you tell
It will be to my grave

In the Past

The past comes back to you
In some way or another
It's how you chose
To deal with it is the answer

How do you answer a question from long ago
Or how do you deal with the people in that past
You can ignore
Or you can last

When a reminder comes up
You choose that answer
Whether you stand up
Or run faster

Either way
It's time
To deal with it today
Regardless of the time

Fair Game

I have no control
You have taken my worst
You have taken my soul
What could be worse

Never have you said the words
Never have you reached out
It's a double edge sword
I have no doubt

I have sought love
For approval
For something new
And never the unusual

You have me wrapped in knots
My guilt and my shame
Is what cost me the lot
But for you, it's fair game

Say it Isn't So

My arms open
You are mistaken
\For you to focus
But it's broken

For so many years
You have owned me
Somehow, someway you have to hear
That what was the key

The key to my life
But why am I taking it back
Because you see if
I let that happen I would be a maniac

You would not matter
In some way, you have to go
Whether it is sadden
It could only be so

Sunny

As we go around on this merry-go-round
Called life
People get off and people get on
You determine how long the ride

As you get older
Those people come and go
But the ones that stay are the ones that matter
Cuz you have to grow

We welcome each and every one
It's how you treat each other
Should know-how
Is to have one another

My life is not rich
Not by money
But by the list
Because life will always be sunny

Doubt

We always say
Our thoughts and prayers are with you
Is that the way
Through the sorrow

I question that
Because our lives go on
I have said
We are the black swan

You're always surrounded
Whether it be people by distractions or just you
We were not meant to be so blinded
I think I'm better off though

Can we go on without you
Yes we can
And we have
It can't go back to where we began

We go from here
How that turns out
Who knows, but we have no fear
We will make it, we will make it no doubt

Our Art

My thoughts race
Why you and not her
I'm trying to remember each part of your face
Please I don't care

She's everything
Her laugh, smile, and unconditional love
Going out on an angels wing
And watching from above

Your heart so inviting
Your arms always open
Every talk so exciting
All of us hoping

You can't take her
Not now I am begging
Our lives unfair
Because she is so loving

Love knows no time
Only hearts
Why can't it be a nursery rhyme
So we can keep the master of your art

Final Days

I can't turn it off
I can't seem to find a thought
We are on this merry-go-round of life
Can we get off or not

Cause Lord knows I want a do-over
Hers, his, mine, what are we waiting for
Because in life it's forever
So why would we want more

The what if's
Or the why not
Doesn't matter 'cause it's all a gift
So why would we want more

In my final days
I want my family and friends
To say cause it takes
everything to make it to the end

Brokered

If we could turn back time
Would you
If so would you flip it on a dime
Or would you slow it down

Take me at my word
I would flip in a second
But it would become a blur
Or just a complete wreck

We live our lives as if we had forever
So why can it be like that
As we fight all together
Our battle may fall flat

Her battle has ended
We must go forward
Our suffering uncomprehended
Your peace has been brokered

Apology

You have let me down at every turn
Why should I try
I let you in just to get burned
Because as you see I have no more to cry

They say two out of three ain't bad
But when you are number three
It is very sad
She has her apology

What do I have
Not one thing
Not even half
It's not because I don't cling

However, does she even bother
I think not
Because she has hers to smother
And I never had a spot

Brave

You split me into
But you made me whole
If it were up to you
I would be so full

We have each other
But I need you more
So you would rather
Go out the front door

I tried and tried
But never did I succeed
Go with it on stride
And always in need

Need your trust
But needing your love
I must
Show your kind of

The kind of touch
I thought I gave
But realized you must
Have to be brave

Day Dream

I watched as you went
Not wanting you to go
Feeling out of place even when
We would always have a home

Many years ago we daydreamed so big
But for it to come true
We had to dig
Dig so far through

As we exhausted all avenues
My heart broke
I felt so confused
But all I could do is choke

Choke back the tears
I didn't want you to see
Only because I wouldn't bear
Bear the thought you never feel

Feel the love I have always had
Then and now
It seems so sad
But if someday, somehow

Our daydream could be
If only for a minute
We would always see
That perfect life for us on target

My Plea

I can only imagine how
How it is and how it could be
And only now
I needed to see

See you in the next years
See into the future
I am brought to tears
Because I am sure

Sure it will never change
Only you
You have that chain
The chain that cripples a few

But see your chains doesn't hold me
Or cripple me
My God I plea
That you see me on my knees

I may not be carefree
And I may not be ideal
But you don't own me
I will heal

Us

You were there when I was in need
My love for you I cannot describe
But know it will always be
That our love thrived

If only I could
Change what I had
I could have always been loved

As you walked out
All I could feel
Was the love out loud
That both our lives are fulfilled

We live our lives
Like it was scripted
We both have a different life
With all of it a gift

As with everyone
You are cautious
But from day one
It wasn't you and I, but for us

Only You

Our journey in life is not mapped out
How do we manage
What if I shout
Would that give me the advantage

I want the time back
So please tell me how that can be
In my mind, it's all black
How can I see

My map seems off
The twists and turns
Are not a trade-off
But it is on someone else's terms

When my journey ends
My life will be whole
Because in my life I had many friends
But only you had my soul

Baby Girl

I know you are looking down
wondering why
why the frown
I want the reason for what, when, and why

Your love was always there
whether you told me or not
I could always bear
but now I'm caught

It would make you sad
because you would always say
baby girl it's not that bad
you will have your day

My time is near
yours is gone
what do I fear
I guess it would being alone

Your baby girl is gonna make it
come hell or high water
my candle is lit
so I will hold it higher

Exhale

When does life finally give
Is it when you give up
Or is it when you give in
But either way, it is up to us

He gave us light
He gave us love
Is it in your sights
I don't know if it's sort of

Does it have to be one or the other
Or can it be both
Because I feel so smothered
Up and under the growth

I want the pain to stop
How can that be
If life never puts you on top
All we can do is believe

Without You

The days move on without you
How can I
I have to
Even though I don't know-how

Life is so hard
Without you
My mind races and keeps me off guard
How do I keep from falling through

Our lives are so different
Without you
Every move deliberate
If you only knew

For some reason
I already know you do
Why can't it be even
Without you

Her Shore

You're crystal clear
But the twists and turns are unseen
I want to be so near
However, it's what is deemed

Your Sandy beaches
And Rocky coves
So far-reaching
We all love

You have taken
As well as given
The sun comes up and you awaken
You are never driven

The waves crash
The current so fast
It can't be bought with cash
Though it can be asked

It will take everything
But give even more
Every passing spring
She will show you her Shore

See All

Why do we do what we do
Some of us are driven
Be it by you
Or by it given

You tell me daily
If not for you
So why can't you say
For you I do

Would it be a lie
Or what you tell yourself
Either way, I sigh
Because you see we are all left

Why are you different
You see you're not
Whether you think it
You've not been forgot

I have been told
He hears and sees all
We don't wear a damn blindfold
But behind the eight-ball

Apart

The look in his eyes is endless
How do we fill his dreams
Do we in mindless
Or do we let him bust at the seams

He looks to us for guidance
For love
To look over the horizon
He needs all of us from above

Our love for him is undeniable
As with my boys
But for him it is justifiable
The rest of it is background noise

To my dying day
He has my heart
So I say
To you, he is set apart

Withdrawn

Your pain I will never know
They left one by one
In your eyes, they left you
Though there will always be someone

Your trust unbreakable
Your loyalty incomparable
It's unmistakable
It is so admirable

People come and go
You never have
We think we have known
However, we don't know half

As life goes on
We lose this one and that one
You became so withdrawn
But you could never be outdone

Please God

My life goes on every day
As if you were never here
What can I say
It's like you just disappeared

Putting one foot in front of the other
Is about all I can do
There could never be another
Why did it have to be you

I sit and ponder
How do I go from here
All I can do is wonder
Your voice is all I want to hear

Please God
I beg
It feels so odd
I wish someone was pulling

His Art

I look into your eyes
All I see is wonder
We are wise
You just want to feel the thunder

We want to hear your laughter
Because you see
It's him you take after
You can clearly see

He has my heart
Through and through
His art
Is our glue

It seems as if we are fractured
But we're not
We can't have it manufactured
So why not a hook

ABOUT THE AUTHOR

Debbi Brawner has two children that have challenged and inspired
her in every way over her 5 year writing career. She has lived in
the same small country town in the Mid-South all her life. Her
children and rural neighborly environment have brought to fruition
this collection of growth, healing, love, grief, and self-awareness.
In the last year, there have been many whirlwind changes to her
life but they were much needed.
Debbi takes great pride in re-releasing her first book of poetry
previously published as "If Not Me, The Who?"

www.ingramcontent.com/pod-product-compliance
Lightning Source LLC
Chambersburg PA
CBHW061333120726
48001CB00002B/839